SIMPSONS

COMICS

STRIKE BACK!

Titan Books

To the loving memory of Snowball I:
You may be gone, but the mice
still fear for their lives.

Published in the UK by Titan Books Ltd., 42-44 Dolben Street,
London SE1 OUP, under licence from Bongo Entertainment, Inc.

FIRST EDITION: DECEMBER 1996

ISBN 1-85286-764-7

98 99 00 RRD   4 6 8 10 9 7 5 3

Publisher: MATT GROENING
Managing Editor: JASON GRODE
Art Director / Editor: BILL MORRISON
Book Design: MARILYN FRANDSEN
Legal Guardian: SUSAN GRODE

Contributing Artists:
PETER ALEXANDER, TIM BAVINGTON, SHARON BRIDGEMAN,
SHAUN CASHMAN, JEANNINE CROWELL, STEPHANIE GLADDEN,
TIM HARKINS, NATHAN KANE, BILL MORRISON,
DAVID MOWRY, PHIL ORTIZ, CHRIS ROMAN, CHRIS UNGAR

Contributing Writers:
ADAM FEIN, TERRY DELEGEANE, SCOTT M. GIMPLE, GARY GLASBERG,
ANDREW GOTTLIEB, CLAY GRIFFITH, BILL MORRISON, JEFF ROSENTHAL,
SCOTT SHAW!, MARY TRAINOR, LONA WILLIAMS

Printed in Italy

CONTENTS

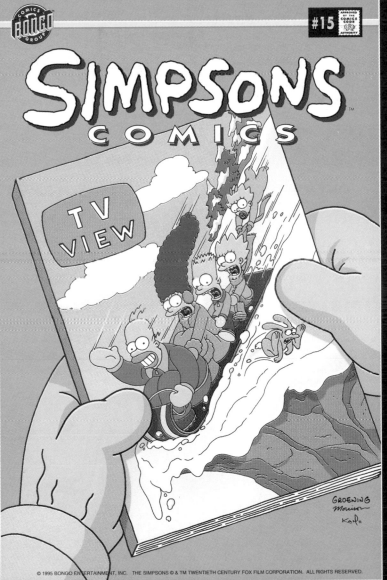

LISA'S TOP FORTY: 1. My baritone saxophone. *2. The Happy Little Elves as a group.* **3. The Happy Little Elves individually: a. Yendor. b. Bubbles. c. Doofy. d. Moldy.** 4. The joy of overachievement. **5. Finding a surprise dessert in my lunchbox.** 6. Bleeding Gums Murphy. 7. Tetherball. *8. Seeing Bart get caught red-handed.* **9. Cartoons with redeeming social messages.** *10. Looking on the bright side.* 11. Be-bop. 12. Playing both sides against the middle. **13. My friend Janey. 14. Corn-on-the-cob. 15. Television.** *16. The way my baby sister smells right after her bath.* **17. The pursuit of happiness.** *18. Recess.* **19. The time I got all 50 states playing the "License Plate Game" on our trip to Hell Valley National Park.** 20. Any form of revenge on Bart. **21. Expressing my inner howl through music.** 22. Mom's cooking. **23. Moral superiority as a lifestyle.** *24. Amelia Earhart.* **25. Those sprinkle things that go on top of ice cream and cupcakes.** *26. The (imagined) delight of getting a pony for Christmas.* 27. Snowball II. **28. Santa's Little Helper.** 29. Freedom of choice. *30. A Super-Deluxe Krusty Burger with bacon, chili, cheese and extra Krusty Secret Sauce.* **31. Ms. Hoover...on a good day. 32. Mr. Bergstrom any time.** 33. My dad's laugh. *34. Peace.* 35. The painful beauty of Emily Dickinson's verse. **36. Being a misunderstood creative genius.** 37. Daffodils. **38. Angst.** 39. Putting on a brave front. *40. And, in spite of everything, my family.*

HEY, MAN! WHAT HAPPENED TO THE ELECTRICITY?

AAAA-AAAAH!

NO TV!!! CHRISTMAS IS RUINED!

AH, WHAT ARE YOU ALL BELLY-ACHING ABOUT? WHY, *NERTZ*, BACK IN *MY* DAY WE DIDN'T EVEN *HAVE* TV!

:GASP!:

OH MY *GOSH!*

THAT'S *RIGHT!* OL' SATAN HADN'T GOT AROUND TO IN-VENTING IT YET!

IMAGINE *THAT!* CHRISTMAS WITHOUT *TELEVISION!*

OOOOOOOOHHHHHHH!

:SHUDDER:

SO TELL US, GRAMPA, WHAT WAS IT LIKE BACK THEN?

YEAH, GRAMPA.... TELL US ABOUT WHEN *YOU* WERE A KID!

YES, GRAMPA. I THINK THE CHILDREN SHOULD HEAR HOW LIFE WAS *BEFORE* TELEVISION.

BEFORE TV STOLE OUR SOULS AWAY FROM US, YOU MEAN! *DEVILVISION*, I CALL IT! EXCEPT FOR MATLOCK, OF COURSE. MARK MY WORDS, WE'LL HAVE *BEELZEBUB* TO PAY FOR THIS...

YEAH, YEAH, GRAMPS... WE'RE ALL GONNA BURN IN HELL FOR WATCHING *TOP COPS!* WE GET THE PICTURE. NOW TELL US ABOUT WHEN YOU WERE A KID.

WELL, ALRIGHT THEN...

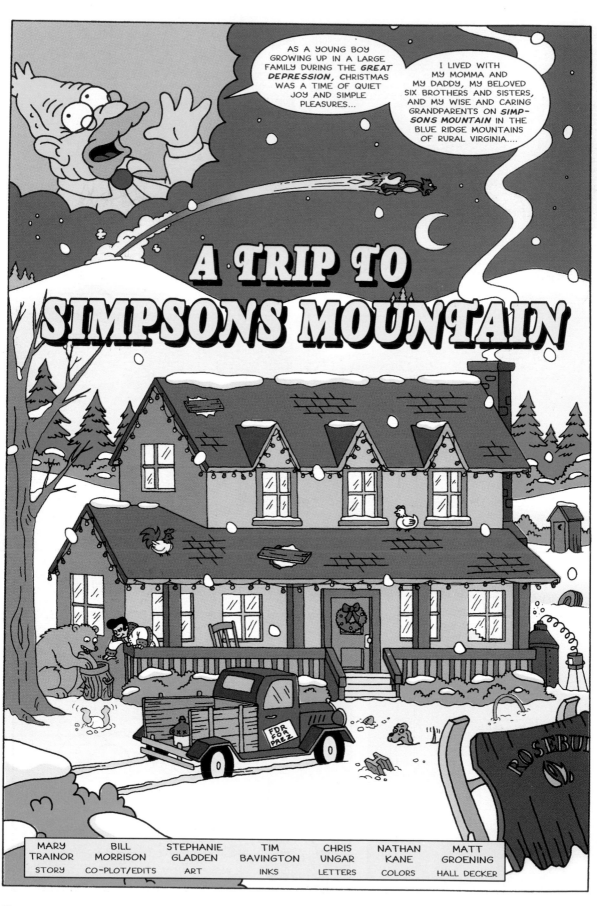

A TRIP TO SIMPSONS MOUNTAIN

OUR FAMILY'S MODEST INCOME CAME FROM A *SAW MILL* THAT MY DADDY RAN WITH *GRAMPA ZEKE*...

LOOK OUT, YOU DERN *FOOL!* YOU'RE GONNA CUT OFF YOUR...

D'OH!!!

OURS WAS A LARGE BUT CLOSE-KNIT AND LOVING FAMILY...

LANDSAKES! I WISH THEY'D INVENT SOMETHING TO KEEP KIDS SITTING IN ONE PLACE...MAYBE SOME KIND OF *BOX* THAT *LIGHTS UP,* YOU KNOW... AND MAKES *SOUNDS*...

MOMMA, YOU'RE BABBLING. ARE YOU HAVING ONE OF YOUR *SPELLS?* YOU WANT ME TO FETCH YOUR *RE-LAXING MEDICINE?*

XXX

MOMMA HAD HER HANDS FULL WITH ALL THOSE YOUNG-'UNS, BUT SHE COULD ALWAYS TURN TO *GRANDMA ZZA-ZZA* FOR SUPPORT...

DAHLINK, *REALLY!* I'D *LUFF* TO HELP YOU OUT, BUT ALL YOUR ZILLY LITTLE CHILDREN ARE CHUST TOO, TOO *BORING!*

I REMEMBER IN PARTICULAR THIS ONE YEAR. IT WAS *CHRISTMAS EVE* AND MY DADDY HAD GONE WAY UP ON SIMPSONS MOUNTAIN TO FETCH US BACK A *CHRISTMAS TREE!*

♫ OH, NINETY-NINE BOTTLES OF BEER ON THE WALL, NINETY-NINE BOTTLES OF BEER... ♪

HE HAD LEFT EARLY THE DAY BEFORE AND HADN'T COME BACK YET...

VAIT! ABE! I NEED NEW *PEDALS* FOR MY *EXERCYCLE!* DO BE A DAHLINK AND ZTOP ON YOUR WAY AND GET ME SOME, WON'T YOU?

YOU KNOW, GRANDPA, THIS SOUNDS *AWFULLY* FAMILIAR. DIDN'T WE SEE THIS ON *TV?*

GREAT BALD-HEADED *JUPITER!* I *TOLD* YOU, THIS WAS *BEFORE TV!*

WELL, IF IT WAS *BEFORE* TV, HOW COME YOUR FAMILY HAD *OPENING CREDITS?*

WILL YOU SHUT UP AND LET ME FINISH...

LIKE I WAS SAYING, MY DADDY AIN'T BEEN BACK YET, AND MOMMA WAS PRETTY NEAR SICK WITH WORRY...

AND SO, I SET OFF TO FIND MY DADDY. I PASSED THE HOME OF THE ECCENTRIC *BALDWIN SISTERS*...

TRUDGE TRUDGE TRUDGE TRUDGE

LOOK, IT'S THAT WHITE TRASH *ABE-BOY SIMPSON*. EVERY *CHRISTMAS EVE* HIS DADDY GOES OFF ON A BENDER AND *OLIDIA* SENDS THAT FOOL KID OUT LOOKING FOR HIM.

GOODNESS GRACIOUS. PEOPLE LIKE THAT GIVE *DRINKING* A BAD NAME.

YES, SISTER. THAT'S WHY WE MUST TAKE CARE TO SHARE OUR "RECIPE" WITH ONLY THE FINER FOLKS IN THIS TOWN...

...THE ONES WITH THE CHARM AND BREEDING TO BE ALCOHOLICS...NOT MERE DRUNKARDS!

OH, AND LOOK, SISTER. HERE COMES OUR OWN *REVEREND REED*!

LET'S GET OUT THE GOOD CRYSTAL 8-OUNCE TUMBLERS, SHALL WE?

DURING *THE GREAT DEPRESSION,* MOMMA AND THE CHILDREN WERE SOMETIMES ABLE TO *SUPPLEMENT* OUR FAMILY'S MODEST *INCOME* BY TOURING THE COUNTRY *LIP-SYNCING* INSIPID, *WHITE-BREAD* ROCK MUSIC.

PUTTA- PUTTA- PUT!

I KNEW MOMMA WAS COUNTING ON ME AND THAT RESPONSIBILITY BEGAN TO WEIGH HEAVY ON MY SPIRITS.

VRRROOOM!

ABE, MY MAN! WHY SO GLUM, BRO?

HEY, *JASON*, *LUKE* AND *TORI-MAE*! MOMMA SENT ME OUT TO FETCH DADDY BACK, AND I CAN'T FIND HIM!

OH, MAN. I *FEEL* YOUR *PAIN*.

LUKE, LIKE, *TOTALLY* KNOWS WHAT PAIN *IS*.

WELL, CHECK IT OUT, *ABE-STER*. WE'RE MEETING *BRENDA* AND *KELLY-SUE* AT THE *TAR PIT*. WANNA HANG WITH US?

GEE, I'D LIKE TO, BUT I CAN'T LET MOMMA DOWN. THAT WOULD BREAK HER HEART.

HEAR YOU, DUDE. *I* FEEL MOMMA'S PAIN, *TOO*!

LUKE IS THE *KING* OF PAIN.

HE IS THE *ANGST-A-GANGSTA*! MY MAIN MAN!

WELL, I GOTTA GET GOING, GUYS. IF I DON'T FIND DADDY SOON THERE'LL BE NO CHRISTMAS ON SIMPSONS MOUNTAIN.

ER ARRG

OH, MAN. *NO CHRISTMAS!* I AM IN *SO* MUCH *PAIN!*

FWAP!

OOOPS, SORRY, LUKE! I DIDN'T MEAN TO *UPSET* YOU!

OH, WOW! I'M GONNA GO HOME AND GET DRUNK AND MOPE AROUND AND GET OUT MY GUN AND SHOOT OUT MY STEREO AND THEN BREAK UP WITH MY GIRLFRIEND AND GIVE MY-SELF A NEAR-LETHAL DOSE OF TRIPLE EXPRESSO CAFÉ LATTÉ AND MOPE AROUND SOME MORE AND THEN DRIVE MY VINTAGE PORSCHE SPEEDSTER OFF OF A CLIFF, MAN!

OOOOH! SOUNDS, LIKE, *UTTERLY TRAGIC,* LUKE. BUT CAN YOU, LIKE DROP US OFF AT THE TAR PIT FIRST?

HEY, NO PROBLEM.

VRRROOOM!

MAN, I KNOW WE'RE IN THE MIDDLE OF *THE GREAT DEPRES-SION*, BUT THAT GUY IS *REALLY* DEPRESSING!

FEELING IN NEED OF A TONIC TO LIFT MY SPIRITS, I STOPPED INTO *IKE GODFREY'S* GENERAL STORE FOR A ROOT BEER...

THIS END UP

UH, HELLO, IKE...BOY, YOU SURE HAVE *CHANGED* THE OLD PLACE!

YES. YES. YOU *BET!* I AM THOROUGHLY *MODERNIZED* NOW!

HI DIDDLY HO, BART!

MY NAME IS *ABE-BOY*, SIR.

NOW, NOW, SON. RESPECT YOUR ELDERS.

WOULD YOU CARE TO AVAIL YOURSELF OF OUR NEW SQUISHEE MACHINE?

ALTHOUGH IKE'S REMODELING HAD MADE THE STORE UNRECOGNIZABLE TO ME, AND HIS PRICES WERE ASTRONOMICALLY *HIGH* FOR 1937, I FELT ODDLY AT HOME IN THESE STRANGE SURROUNDINGS.

SLURP!

...ONE MINI-BAG PORK RINDS, $1.29; ONE SIX-PAK DUFF BEER, $3.25; TWO FROZEN CORN-DOG COMBO MEALS, $6.95...

HAVE A NICE DAY!

?

THAT'S TOTALLY UNBELIEVABLE, GRAMPA. BUT AT *LEAST* IT DOESN'T SOUND LIKE SOMETHING I'VE SEEN ON *TV!*

I DON'T KNOW WHAT WAS IN THAT SQUISHEE, BUT SUDDENLY, ALL THE COLOR DRAINED FROM MY VISION.

THEODORE!

THEODORE...*BEAVER!* YOU ANSWER ME WHEN I CALL YOU, YOUNG MAN!

BUT, I'M *ABE-BOY*, MOMMA!

JEEPERS, BEAV! DON'T TALK BACK TO MOM! YOU WANNA GET *CLOBBERED*?

IT'S ALL RIGHT, WALLY... NOW, BEAVER, YOU RUN ALONG AND FIND YOUR FATHER. I HAVE MILK AND COOKIES WAITING FOR YOU AT HOME, DEAR.

YES, MOMMA.

GOLLY, MOM. HE CAN BE SUCH A LITTLE *CREEP* SOMETIMES!

NOW, WALLY...

HOLD IT, GRAMPA! THESE *RE-RUNS* ARE BAD ENOUGH, BUT DO WE HAVE TO HAVE 'EM IN *BLACK AND WHITE*?!

THE BOY'S GOT A POINT THERE. COULDN'T YOU AT LEAST *COLORIZE* 'EM LIKE THAT *TED FONDA* GUY DOES?

THAT'S *TED TURNER*, DAD!

WILL ALL OF YOU BE QUIET AND LET GRAMPA FINISH HIS STORY?

OKAY, BUT IN COLOR, MAN.

I HAD BEGUN TO DESPAIR OF *EVER* FINDING MY DADDY.

AND THEN I SAW A LONE FIGURE STANDING ON A BRIDGE...

PLEASE, *LORD*... I'M SORRY THAT I'D WISHED I'D NEVER BEEN BORN. CLARENCE, *HELP ME!* GET ME *BACK.* I DON'T CARE WHAT HAPPENS TO ME. ONLY GET ME BACK TO MY WIFE AND KIDS! I WANT TO *LIVE* AGAIN!

DADDY? MOMMA SAYS SHE WANTS YOU HOME!

NOW GET OUT OF HERE, BERT, OR I'LL HIT YOU AGAIN! GET OUT.....WHAT? *ABE BOY?* YOU *KNOW* ME, BOY? YOU KNOW WHO I *AM?!*

ZZA-ZZA'S PEDALS! ZZA-ZZA'S...THEY'RE HERE, BERT! WHAT DO YOU KNOW ABOUT THAT! *MERRY CHRISTMAS!*

MOMMA SAYS I'M TO FETCH YOU BACK, DADDY.

WOO-HOO!!!

MERRY CHRISTMAS, SIMPSONS MOUNTAIN! *MERRY CHRISTMAS,* YOU WONDERFUL OL' MOUNTAIN!

OH, GIMME A *BREAK,* GRAMPA! I'VE SEEN *THAT* ON TV A *MILLION TIMES!!*

SHUT UP, BART!!!

25

26

HEINOUS FUNNIES

DECEMBER, 1933

No. 1

BONGO
COMICS GROUP

Featuring
ITCHY & SCRATCHY

AAAAAGGGHH!

COMPL SLAM!

PLEASE! I NEED TO PAY MY FINE TO REMOVE THE DREADED BOOT OF DENVER FROM MY "KWIK-E-MART-SQUISHEE-KART."

COMPLAINTS

BAM BAM

I PROMISE TO NEVER AGAIN SELL FROZEN REFRESHMENTS IN THE EMERGENCY LOADING ZONE OF THE HOSPITAL.

DOORS OPEN AT NINE.

CUSTOMER TIME

ACTUAL TIME

MEANWHILE...

PHOTO STATION

OH, I HOPE ONE OF THE TWO PHOTOS IS FLATTERING.

WHIIRRR!

SNIP!

LUCKY YOU. ONE OF THEM IS.

OFFICIAL SPRINGFIELD DMV

SPRINGFIELD OFFICIAL DMV

YOU'LL RECEIVE YOUR NEW LICENSE IN 4-6 MONTHS. NOW AM-SCRAY!

A MOMENT LATER...

WELL, LET'S LOOK ON THE BRIGHT SIDE. AT LEAST WE'RE OUT OF WORK TOGETHER.

YOU'RE RIGHT. A SMOKE...TO SISTERHOOD.

JEEZUM CROW, IT'S *EMPTY*! SELMA, HOW MANY CIGA-RETTES HAVE YOU *HAD* TODAY?

THE USUAL. ONE HUNDRED AND THIRTY-FIVE SINCE BREAKFAST.

THAT'S STRANGE. WE SHOULD HAVE TWO LEFT.

HRUMPH! FIRST WE LOSE OUR *JOBS*, AND NOW WE'RE OUT OF *CIGARETTES*.

WELL, AT LEAST WE'RE *DONE* WITH IT. REMEMBER, GRANDMA ALWAYS SAID, "BAD LUCK COMES IN *TWO'S*."

THREE'S, PATTY. SHE ONLY SAID *TWO'S* BECAUSE SHE COULDN'T MAKE A *"TH"* SOUND WITHOUT HER *UPPER PLATE* IN.

WE'RE HOME.

43

THAT SAME EVENING...

♪ MAN ON THE LAM ♪ ♪ HE'S A MAN ON THE LAM. NO LAWMAN CAN... ♪ CATCH THE MAN ON THE LAM! ♪

SING IT, HOMER!

WE ALL KNOW HE DIDN'T DO IT, SO WHY DO WE WATCH THE SHOW?

WE'RE ALL AWAITING THE FINAL CONFRONTATION BETWEEN HIM AND THE CLUB-FOOTED GUY.

TONIGHT'S EPISODE: SILENCE OF THE MAN ON THE LAM

HOMER, SOMEONE'S AT THE DOOR. WILL YOU PLEASE GO ANSWER IT?

I THOUGHT CASA DE HUEVOS GRANDE WAS YOUR FAVORITE SHOW.

:DING DONG!:

BUT, MARGE, THIS IS MY FAVORITE SHOW!

THAT'S CHANNEL OCHO! THIS IS MY FAVORITE ONE ON CHANNEL SIX.

I THOUGHT THAT WAS MAKE ROOM FOR PRALINES.

THAT'S ON AT NINE O'CLOCK. THIS IS MY FAVORITE CHANNEL SIX SHOW THAT'S ON RIGHT NOW!

YEAH, OKAY. WHATEVER.

MY GOODNESS, ARE YOU ALRIGHT?

SAVE THE SWEET TALK, LITTLE SISTER. WE'RE FINE.

WE JUST NEED A PLACE TO STAY FOR AWHILE, SOME SMOKES, AND A COUCH TO WATCH MACGYVER ON. YOU WON'T EVEN KNOW WE'RE HERE.

THAT NIGHT...

BART, THANKS FOR SHARING YOUR ROOM WITH ME.

ARE YOU KIDDIN'? I COULDN'T LET YOU SHARE YOUR ROOM WITH AUNT SELMA. THEN I WOULDA' HAD TO SHARE MY ROOM WITH...

:GULP: AUNT PATTY.

IN LISA'S ROOM...

HEY, PATTY, TURN OFF THE NIGHT LIGHT. IT'S BEEN A LONG DAY.

AH, TO SLEEP. PERCHANCE TO DREAM OF CHUCK WOOLERY.

DO NOT TURN OFF. SAPLINGS WILL DIE.

THE NEXT MORNING...

MOM, LOOK! AUNT PATTY AND AUNT SELMA KILLED MY SAPLINGS! I WAS SUPPOSED TO SELL THEM AS A SCHOOL PROJECT FOR EARTH DAY!

I'M SORRY, LISA, I'M SURE THEY DIDN'T MEAN IT.

HERE, HONEY, I'LL BUY THEM FROM YOU... I CAN USE THE... SOIL...FOR...SOMETHING.

YOINK!

SORRY, MARGE! YOU SNOOZE, YOU LOSE!

GLUUMPPH!

AYE, CARUMBA!

45

IT'S *RUINED!*

RADIOACTIVE MAN

BART, I'M VERY SORRY, I'LL GET YOU ANOTHER ONE.

BUT THIS IS THE CLASSIC, ULTRA-RARE, LIMITED EDITION OF *RADIOACTIVE MAN'S NUCLEAR WINTER WONDERLAND – ABSOLUTE ZERO.*

I HAD TO SEND ALL THE WAY TO *PLATTSBURGH* FOR IT. THERE'S NOT ANOTHER ONE ON THIS PLANET!

MEANWHILE IN PLATTSBURGH...

TOP SECRET DO NOT OPEN!

CAUTION: WRATH OF GOD!

RM-NWW-O QUANTITY: 1000 GROSS

WHOOPS!

LATER...

TIME FOR *YOUR* BREAK-FAST, LITTLE TREES.

BRRR... TOO COLD.

MOMENTS LATER...

WOO HOO! BREAKFAST IS *SERVED!*

THE NEXT DAY...

...SO IN SUMMATION, EITHER *THEY* GO, OR *WE* GO! CAN I GET AN *AMEN*, KIDS??

AMEN, DAD!

PREACH IT, HOMER MAN!

I ADMIT, THEY'RE *OBNOXIOUS* AND *UN-GRACIOUS*. BUT THEY'RE MY *SISTERS*. I DON'T KNOW WHAT TO *DO*.

ACK...ACK!

UH, PATTY? SELMA? WE'VE GOT TO TALK.

WE SURE *DO*. THAT DOG OF YOURS *REEKS*!

I WAS THINKING WE COULD TALK ABOUT YOU TWO. YOU KNOW, FINDING NEW *JOBS*, LOOKING FOR AN *APARTMENT*...

THAT'S IT! THEY'RE *OUT* OF HERE!

DO YOU MIND? MACGYVER'S TRAPPED IN AN ABANDONED MINE WITH ONLY HIS WITS, DENTAL FLOSS, AND A TUB OF NON-DAIRY DESSERT TOPPING.

CLICK!

LOOK, I'LL BE BRIEF. YOU TWO NEED TO GET BACK INTO THE WORK FORCE.

A CAREER SHOULD INVOLVE SOMETHING YOU ALREADY ENJOY DOING. SO, FINISH THIS SENTENCE: "I ENJOY..."

SMOKING.

WORKING AT THE DMV.

MAYBE WE SHOULD TRY TO LOOK AHEAD. TRY THIS: "NEXT YEAR AT THIS TIME I WOULD LIKE TO BE..."

SMOKING.

WORKING AT THE DMV.

OKAY, WELL, SOMETIMES IT'S GOOD JUST TO GET OUT OF THE HOUSE FOR A WHILE.

YOU KNOW, CLEAR YOUR HEAD, GET SOME FRESH AIR...

...AND GET OUT OF THE HOUSE! ...FOR AWHILE.

LATER...

OH, YEAH. *MUCH* BETTER.

REVITALIZING.

MAYBE GRANDMA WAS TRYING TO SAY, "BAD LUCK ALWAYS COMES IN *MULTIPLES* OF THREE."

C.M. BURNS CHARTER AIRPORT

AS YOU'LL SEE TO MY IMMEDIATE *LEFT,* AND TO MY *RIGHT,* THERE IS A *PICKET LINE*. PLEASE RETURN TO YOUR CAR AND USE THE EXIT DIRECTLY BEHIND YOU.

YOU WILL BE GIVEN *FIVE SECONDS* TO FIND THE *EXIT* BEFORE WE ASSAULT YOU AND YOUR VEHICLE WITH THESE SIGNS.

°GATE° #10

WE WANT TO BE CALLED FLIGHT COMFORT ENGINEERS

UNFAIR HEIGHT REQUIREMENT

LISTEN, *MS. FRIENDLY THIGHS,* WE NEED WATER FOR THIS CAR.

WE WANT TO BE CALLED FLIGHT COMFORT ENGINEERS

AND WE NEED IT, *NOW!*

UNFAIR HEIGHT REQUIREMENT

I BELIEVE IT'S A KNOT IN YOUR PERFECTLY DEVELOPED *TRAPEZIUS*, SIR.

HELLO, WHAT'S *THIS*?

C.M. BURNS

WAP!

WAP!

NOT *THERE*, YOU NINNY, ON THE *MONITOR*!

WELL, SIR, IT APPEARS THAT TWO MEN DRESSED AS WOMEN ARE PUSHING A LATE MODEL BUICK THROUGH THE MOB OF FLIGHT ATTENDANTS THAT HAVE BEEN PICKETING YOUR AIRLINE.

JUST THINK, SMITHERS. ONE OF THEM COULD DO THE WORK OF *TEN* OF THOSE GLORIFIED, OVERPAID *CAR-HOPS*! MAYBE THEY'RE PART OF A *SUPER RACE* OF FLIGHT ATTENDANTS. I *MUST* HAVE THEM! OFFER THEM JOBS *AT ONCE*!

RIGHT AWAY, SIR.

THAT NIGHT...

ARE YOU *SURE* SMITHERS SAID *FLIGHT ATTENDANTS*? 'CAUSE LENNY SAID THAT THEY WERE LOOKING FOR TWO *CONTAMINATION SHOWER ATTENDANTS*.

LAUGH IT UP, CUE-BALL! LEARNING THE CONTENTS OF THIS MANUAL IS ALL THAT STANDS BETWEEN OUR CAREER IN THE SKY AND LIFE ON EARTH WITH YOU.

AIRLINE SAFETY MANUAL

WOO HOO! *LEARN*, BABY, *LEARN*!

LATER THAT NIGHT...

I WANT TO THANK YOU ALL FOR HELPING MY SISTERS WITH THEIR TRAINING.

I'M GLAD TO DO MY NEIGHBORLY DOODILY-DUTY.

"THE FIRST THING A FLIGHT ATTENDANT SHOULD DO IS WELCOME EVERYONE ABOARD."

AIRLINE SAFETY MANUAL

OKAY, *CHEETAH!* IN WITH THE OTHER CHIMPS!

NICELY!

HAVE A BANANA.

PAT PAT

MAYBE WE SHOULD TRY STARTING WITH SOMETHING THAT INVOLVES *LESS* PASSENGER INTERACTION.

"MAKE SURE ALL CARRY-ON ITEMS ARE STOWED AWAY."

LET ME... *HAVE...* THAT!

BUT I'M *HOLDING* IT SO NOTHING *HAPPENS* TO IT!

THERE, *NOW* IT'S SAFE!

CRUMPF!

HRMMM.

OKAY, IT SAYS HERE, "EVEN DURING TURBULENCE, THE PASSENGER IS ENTITLED TO A NICE HOT OR COLD BEVERAGE."

GUT-B GONE

EEEYAAHH! FIRE DOWN BELOW!

AAAAH! IT'S AS IF I'M BURNING IN ETERNAL HELLFIRE!!

SAY, REVEREND, SHOULDN'T YOU WATCH THE H-E-DOUBLE HOCKEY STICKS IN FRONT OF THE KIDDLES?

CLICK!

LATER...

IT SAYS RIGHT HERE THAT "ALL FLIGHT ATTENDANTS MUST KNOW CPR." YOU MAY NEED TO SAVE A LIFE.

OH, YEAH? WELL, I DON'T THINK POPS HERE IS GOING TO MAKE IT!

HEH, HEH! YEAH. I'LL ONLY SAVE THE CUTE ONES.

HELLO? ...I CAN'T FEEL MY SPINE! HELLO??

HOURS PASS...

BYE-BYE.

TOODLEY-OODLES.

LATER.

LADIES, THERE'LL BE NO LOVE LOST IF I DON'T SEE YOU THIS SUNDAY.

SEE YA.

WHICH WAY TO BAGGAGE CLAIM?

WE DID IT! NOW, ALL WE NEED TO DO IS PASS THE WRITTEN TEST TOMORROW.

PIECE O' CAKE!

THE NEXT DAY...

YOU DID VERY WELL ON THE TESTS, *SISTERS BOUVIER.* YOU BOTH HAD ONLY *ONE* INCORRECT ANSWER.

NUMBER 17, REGARDING LOSS OF CABIN PRESSURE. *INFANTS* ARE ENTITLED TO OXYGEN MASKS, *TOO!*

AND WHICH QUESTION WAS THAT?

YOU LIVE, YOU LEARN.

WELL, CLIMB ABOARD AND *GOOD LUCK!*

EVERY NERVE IN MY BODY IS ON *FIRE.* *FIRE* I TELL YOU, *FIRE!*

I DON'T KNOW HOW MUCH LONGER I CAN *TAKE* THIS, PATTY.

THIS IS TORTURE. SHEER *TORTURE!*

NO SMOKING

FLIGHT ATTENDANTS PREPARE FOR *TAKE-OFF!*

WHEN IS THE CAPTAIN GONNA TURN OFF THAT SIGN?

SOME TIME LATER...

OFF—OFF—OFF—OFF—OFF—OFF—OFF...

NO SMOKING

C'MON, *BABY!* MAMA NEEDS SOME OF THAT SWEET *NIC-O-TINE!*

EXCUSE ME, UH, WE'VE BEEN FLYING FOR *TWO HOURS* AND WE HAVEN'T BEEN SERVED A CUP OF COFFEE.

HECK, WE HAVEN'T EVEN BEEN OFFERED *PEANUTS!*

I'M TERRIBLY SORRY FOR THE DELAY. WHO WOULD LIKE SOME FRESH, HONEY-ROASTED PEANUTS?

SHA-DOINK!

HEADS UP, PEOPLE!

OKAY, WHO WANTS A SOFT DRINK WITH THAT?

COLA

FINE. IF YOU NEED US WE'LL BE TALKING TO THE CAPTAIN.

COCKPIT

C'MON, SELMA, EITHER THE PILOT LANDS THIS PUPPY OR I PUT HIS NOSE INTO AN UPRIGHT AND LOCKED POSITION.

THAT AFTERNOON...

I'M AFRAID OUR DREAMS OF EVER FINDING THAT PERFECT JOB CRASH LANDED ALONG WITH THE PLANE.

LISTEN, I'M SURE YOU TWO WILL FIND A VOCATION THAT'S NOT ONLY FULFILLING, BUT WHERE THERE ARE NO SMOKING RESTRICTIONS.

RING RING

BOB'S ROADKILL JERKY EMPORIUM, YOU MAKE 'EM FLY, WE'LL MAKE 'EM DRY.

I'M SORRY, DAVE, BUT THAT'S NOT POSSIBLE.

DAISY...DAISSSY... GIVE MEEE YOURR ANSSWERRR TRUUUEE...♪♫

GIVE A HOO
DON'T DRINK AND DRIVE

WHAT⁉! UH, LISTEN, I CAN'T HEAR YOU VERY WELL. IT'S A *MADHOUSE* HERE! THE *PRESIDENTS* HAVE GONE *HAYWIRE*, AND NO ONE IS *ANSWERING* THE PHONE AT THE *AUTOMATION CENTER*...

...PLEASE, WE NEED PATTY AND SELMA *RIGHT AWAY*!

PHOTO STATION

REGISTRATION

LATER, AT THE DMV...

CUSTOMER TIME

ACTUAL TIME

...YOU SAID TO FOLLOW THE BLUE LINE, SO I FOLLOWED THE BLUE LINE AND THE LADY THERE ASKED ME WHERE MY FORM IS FROM THE RED LINE...

COMPU

SHA-WAM!

IT'S TOO BAD *GRANDMA* NEVER WORKED AT THE DMV.

WELCOME BACK, SELMA LOVE *Patty*

WELCOME BACK, PATTY LOVE *Selma*

...BUT THERE IS NO RED LINE AND I'VE BEEN IN THIS LINE FOR TWO HOURS...

SHE WOULD HAVE *LOVED* IT. IT'S THE *FOUNTAINHEAD* OF BAD LUCK.

JUST ASK ONE OF OUR *CUSTOMERS!*

HEH, HEH!

THE END

"APU'S INCREDIBLE 96 HOUR SHIFT

(WITHOUT HAVING A BREAK!) "

BILL MORRISON	SHAUN CASHMAN	
SCRIPT	ART	
STARKINGS/ COMICRAFT	ELECTRIC CRAYON	MATT GROENING
LETTERING	COLORS	NIGHT MANAGER

WHAT THE...? THOSE ROTTEN LITTLE *GANGSTERS!* HOW DID *THAT* GET ON HERE?

HOW'S MY SHOPLIFTING? CALL 1-800-GET-BENT!

00:01:19

AH, NOW WE'RE *COOKING WITH GASOLINE!* HERE I AM AT THE START OF MY SHIFT. NOTE MY DAISY FRESH APPEARANCE AND COURTEOUS SMILE.

MY STEADIEST CUSTOMER HAD JUST STOPPED IN FOR A BOX OF DONUTS AND AN IMITATION MICRO-WAVE PORK LOG.

00:03:37

WE WERE IN THE MIDDLE OF A *BUTT-KICKING* SNOW-STORM, AND IN TRADE FOR HIS SNACK TREATS, MISTER HOMER OFFERED TO CLEAR MY PARKING LOT WITH HIS SNOW PLOW.

00:05:52

HERE YOU SEE ONE OF MY MOST *UNTRUSTWORTHY* CUSTOMERS, RECENTLY ESCAPED FROM PRISON, ENTERING THE STORE. WHAT YOU ARE ABOUT TO WITNESS IS AN ACT OF SAVAGE, STOMACH-STRANGLING BRUTALITY, SO PLEASE...

00:06:11

...PAY *CLOSE* ATTENTION!

00:06:32

I DON'T KNOW WHAT CAME OVER ME. MAYBE I WAS POSSESSED BY THE SPIRITS OF ALL THE BULLET-RIDDEN, KWIK-E-MART EMPLOYEES WHO WENT BEFORE ME...

LOOK! A DEFENSELESS OLD WOMAN WITH A BROKEN ARM, AND A POCKETBOOK BULGING WITH HUNDRED DOLLAR BILLS!

HUH? *WHERE?*

00:06:40

...OR MAYBE IT WAS TOO MUCH COFFEE.

CHUTNEY

SKLUTCH!

TAKE *THAT* AND TELL ME HOW YOU *LIKE* IT!

YEEAARGH! OH, MAN! THIS FULLY *BITES!*

SLOOSH!

PREPARE TO BE SEVERELY PUMMELED ABOUT THE HEAD AND SHOULDER AREA!!

ANYHOW, AS YOU ARE SEEING, I HAMMERED THE HOLY *SNOT* OUT OF THAT GUY!

THWOK!

00:06:52

NEXT, I CALLED 911 AND WAITED FOR THE POLICE TO ARRIVE. BY THE WAY, WHEN YOU HAVE *YOUR* FIRST HOLD-UP, YOU NEED NOT WASTE TIME DIALING ALL THREE NUMBERS. WE HAVE IT ON OUR *SPEED-DIAL* SYSTEM.

00:11:17

HERE I AM A FEW MOMENTS LATER.

MR. HOMER! LOOK WHAT YOU HAVE BEEN *DOING!* YOU HAVE PLOWED ME UNDER WITH MY OWN SNOW! *COME BACK,* MR. HOMER!

♪ CALL MR. PLOW, THAT'S THE NAME! THAT NAME AGAIN IS MR. PLOW! ♪

00:21:14

I SUDDENLY REALIZED THAT I WAS *TRAPPED* IN THE STORE WITH A *VICIOUS KILLER,* AND NO *FOOD!*

00:21:21

BUT UNCLE APU, WHAT ABOUT THE HEAT LAMP DOGS AND THE NACHO CHIPS WITH SYNTHETIC CHEESE-COVERING?

TSK, TSK. HOW SOON YOU SEEM TO BE FORGETTING LESSON 12 -- "FOOD FROM *KWIK-E* CAN MAKE YOU *SICKY.*"

AH, YES. I AM *CHAGRINED.*

ANYHOW, IT WAS BEFORE TOO LONG WHEN I HEARD THE VOICE OF CHIEF OF POLICE WIGGUM CALLING TO ME ON A BULL'S HORN FROM OUTSIDE.

MR. NAHASAPEEMAPETILON, YOU'VE BARRICADED YOURSELF *IN!* IS ANYTHING *WRONG?*

I HAVE BEEN *PLOWED* IN. PLEASE LOCATE MR. HOMER AND TELL HIM TO UNPLOW ME!

OKAY, BUT IT MAY TAKE SOME TIME. CAN YOU SEND OUT SOME COFFEE AND DONUTS?

YOU INCOMPETENT *NINCOMPOOP!* I CANNOT OPEN MY *DOOR!*

OH, GOTCHA! SITUATION UNDERSTOOD.

NOW DON'T PANIC! I BELIEVE THERE *MAY* BE AN OPEN DONUT SHOP NEARBY!

I BEGAN TO SEE THAT I WAS GOING TO HAVE SOME EXTRA TIME ON MY HANDS, SO I INDULGED IN SOME PLEASANT DIVERSIONS.

YEAH, SURE WE DO.

HELLO, MOE'S BAR? I WOULD LIKE TO KNOW IF YOU HAVE *OLD GRANDAD* IN A BOTTLE.

00:54:16

⊱TEE HEE HEE⊰ OLD GRANDAD IN A BOTTLE... ⊱WEE HEE⊰ WHAT AN *AUDACIOUS* JOKE I HAVE PLAYED! ⊱HAW HAW⊰

HELLO?... HELLO?... WHAT THE HECK IS SO FUNNY?... HELLO?

00:54:20

MANY HOURS PASSED, AND I BEGAN HAVING TROUBLE STAYING ALERT.

SO TELL ME, MISTER TRAVOLTA, WHAT WAS IT LIKE TO BE DANCING WITH UMA THURMAN IN YOUR FICTITIOUS *PULP* MOVIE?

WHAT? WHERE?

10:46:48

BUT WHY DID YOU NOT TAKE A NAP?

A KWIK-E-CLERK *NEVER* DESERTS HIS POST! ESPECIALLY NOT WHEN THERE IS A DANGEROUS CRIMINAL ON THE PREMISES.

I REMAINED AWAKE BY KEEPING MYSELF BUSY! SEE, HERE I AM CLEANING OUT THE SQUISHEE MACHINE.

11:59:07

HMM...PERHAPS I SHOULD HAVE CLEANED THIS THING OUT AFTER MY *KENTUCKY-FRIED SQUISHEE* EXPERIMENT.

THE LONGER I WAS STAYING AWAKE, THE STRANGER MY ACTIVITIES WERE BECOMING.

A SHRINE TO *GANEESHA* MADE ENTIRELY FROM *BEEF JERKY!*

I WOULD LIKE TO SEE REVEREND LOVEJOY TOP *THIS!*

THE STRANGER MY ACTIONS BECAME, THE LESS I AM REMEMBERING THEM.

LOOK AT ME! I'M CIRCUS BOY! WEEE!

36:15:42

I CAN DO THAT, I CAN DO THAT! THAT I CAN DOOOO!

72:18:23

AT LAST, SALVATION CAME BURSTING THROUGH MY FRONT DOOR.

LEMME AT' EM!

WHERE ARE THEY?

96:01:37

THERE HE IS, COLLAPSED IN THAT PORK-RIND DISPLAY!

LET'S JUST PRAY TO GOD, HE DIDN'T CRUSH 'EM ALL.

BROTHER APU! ARE YOU ALL RIGHT?

"AT LAST, MY SHIFT HAD ENDED!"

BZZ...BZZ...THE FLOWERS ARE CALLING OUT TO ME...BZZ...THERE IS MUCH WORK TO BE DONE...AND I'M JUST THE LITTLE HUMMINGBIRD WHO CAN DO IT!

QUICKLY! SOMEBODY GET THIS MAN SOME NECTAR!

OH, YEAH! I CAN BREATHE AGAIN!

I THINK MY LUNGS WERE BEGINNING TO LOSE THEIR COATING OF TAR!

HEAVEN FORBID!

THANK YOU FOR RESCUING ME, BUT 96 HOURS IS NOT EXACTLY A SPEEDY RESPONSE TIME!

OH, DON'T THANK ME.

IT WOULD HAVE TAKEN LONGER IF THE BOUVIER SISTERS HADN'T RUN OUT OF CIGARETTES. IT SEEMS THAT YOUR STORE IS THE ONLY ONE IN TOWN THAT STOCKS THEIR BRAND -- LADY LARAMIE, FILTER-FREE WITH 40% MORE TAR. THEY TUNNELED THROUGH THAT SNOW IN NO TIME FLAT. NOW, ABOUT THOSE DONUTS...

SO THERE YOU HAVE YOUR LESSON FOR TODAY!

STOP

BUT WHAT HAVE I LEARNED, UNCLE APU?

THAT EVEN IF YOU WORK FOR 96 HOURS WITHOUT A SINGLE SALE, YOUR TIME SPENT WORKING IS NEVER A WASTE.

ESPECIALLY IF YOU HAVE A COUSIN WHO WORKS ON THE TV SHOW "AMERICA'S STRANGEST SECURITY CAMERA VIDEOS." TWENTY THOUSAND DOLLAR GRAND PRIZE, COME TO PAPA!

THE END

WHAT'S THE FREQUENCY, SIMPSON?

COME HERE, YOU LITTLE... WHEN YOU'VE GOT *HOMER SIMPSON* AS AN ENEMY, YOU'RE IN A WORLD OF TROUBLE. *HEY,* QUIT FIGHTING DIRTY!

SCRIPT	PENCILS	INKS	LETTERS	COLORS	MR. TELEVISION
ANDREW GOTTLIEB	PHIL ORTIZ	TIM BAVINGTON	JEANNINE CROWELL	NATHAN KANE	MATT GROENING

BOY! IS IT BETTER YET?!

A LITTLE TO THE LEFT! TRY BENDING IT UP MORE!

BART, STOP TORMENTING YOUR FATHER.

COME ON, MOM. THIS IS THE ONLY WAY I CAN CONTROL THE REMOTE.

I CONTROL THE VERTICAL! I CONTROL THE HORIZONTAL!

CLICK!

CLICK!

CLICK!

HELLO, I'M TROY MCCLURE. PERHAPS YOU REMEMBER ME FROM OTHER TRAVEL SHOWS SUCH AS, "WHERE THE HECK IS THE PEOPLE'S REPUBLIC OF KAMPUCHEA?" AND "BOY, OH CHEBOYGAN!"...

EYE ON SPRINGFIELD

CLICK!

KENT BROCKMAN HERE, AND IF I DIDN'T KNOW BETTER, I'D SAY THAT THIS NEXT SENSATIONAL STORY IS ABSOLUTELY TRUE...

CLICK!

HI, EVERYBODY!

TODAY WE'RE GOING TO LEARN ABOUT MY LATEST NEW MIRACLE INVENTION: "H30"-- THE WETTEST WATER YOU EVER TASTED!...

HI, DR. NICK!

WHOA! YOU CAN RENT OUT A WHOLE TV CHANNEL? LIKE IT WAS A CAR OR A GUN OR SOMETHING?

WELL, MORE LIKE A CAR. IT'S PROBABLY A VERY SMALL PUBLIC ACCESS STATION THAT ONLY BROAD-CASTS TO SPRINGFIELD.

COOL!

THIS CHANNEL FOR RENT

HI-DIDDILY-HO, NEIGHBOR. FINALLY TAKING DOWN THAT OLD DINOSAUR, I SEE.

IF YOU *MUST* KNOW, FLANDERS, THIS IS AN *ANTENNA* AND I'M TRYING TO FIX THE *RECEPTION!*

RECEPTION? WELL, NOT THAT I MIND, BUT YOU'VE BEEN SPLICING INTO MY *CABLE LINE* FOR *YEARS* NOW!

YOU DON'T *NEED* AN ANTENNA!

D'OH!!

...THOUGH I *WOULD* LIKE MY WIRE CUTTERS BACK.

THE BOY... MUST PUNISH THE BOY...

YEEARRRRGH!!!

BART! YOU ALMOST *KILLED* ME UP THERE!

UH, OH!

I CAN'T WAIT TO SEE WHAT THE KRUSTY-DUDE'S GOING TO DO NEXT.

ME, EITHER. I GOT A SWEET TOOTH FOR THIS STUFF.

BAM! BAM!

WOW, I CAN'T BELIEVE I'VE FINALLY OUTGROWN THE OLD "PIE-IN-THE-FACE" BIT.

HEY, PUT SOMETHING ELSE ON! SOMETHING NEW THAT'LL HELP US REDISCOVER OUR LOVE AFFAIR WITH TV!

DID YOU HEAR THAT, LIS? THAT'S THE SOUND OF A RESTLESS VIEWING PUBLIC. AND DO YOU KNOW WHAT WE SHOULD DO WHEN WE HEAR THAT SOUND?

NO. WE SHOULD FIND OUT ABOUT RENTING THAT PUBLIC ACCESS TV CHANNEL.

IGNORE IT AND KEEP GOING TO THE COMIC STORE?

IT'S NOT THAT SIMPLE, BART. PUBLIC ACCESS TELEVISION IS ONE OF THE MOST DEMOCRATIC EXPRESSIONS OF FREE SPEECH AVAILABLE IN THE COUNTRY. ITS DEGENER-ATION AND MISUSE IS TRULY A NATIONAL TRAGEDY.

COMEDY, TRAGEDY... WHAT'S THE DIFFERENCE, AS LONG AS IT'S ENTERTAINING!

MANAGER

EXCUSE ME, BUT IS IT TRUE THAT YOU HAVE A TV CHANNEL FOR RENT?

THAT DEPENDS. ARE YOU PLANNING ON PROGRAMMING SOME KIND OF *SMUT*?

OF *COURSE* NOT!

OH... WELL, I'LL RENT IT TO YOU ANYWAY.

HOW MUCH?

HOW MUCH YOU GOT?

SIXTEEN DOLLARS AND HALF A PACK OF TROPICAL FRUIT-FLAVORED CHEWING GUM.

GOT ANY *STRAUBLE-BLAZZBERRY* IN THERE?

I THINK SO.

IT'S A *DEAL*. YOU'RE ON THE AIR IN FIFTEEN MINUTES.

BUT WHAT'LL WE *DO*? WE'RE NOT PREPARED OR ANYTHING.

YOINK!

USE WHATEVER WE GOT IN BACK. KNOCK YOURSELVES OUT.

FLOUR

WHIPPED CREAM

MANAGER

EYE ON ~NGFIELD

YES, IT'S TRUE. *SIMP-TV* --THAT TAWDRY, FLY-BY-NIGHT NEW CHANNEL--SEEMS TO BE GATHERING FANS AMONG SPRINGFIELD'S MARGINAL AND DISENFRANCHISED. BUT *THIS* REPORTER PREDICTS *SIMP-TV* WILL BE NOTHING MORE THAN A FLASH IN THE PAN.

YOU GUYS HAVE TO *DO* SOMETHING! SIMP-TV IS KICKING OUR *BUTTS!* I HAVE A *MORTGAGE,* YOU KNOW!

CALM DOWN, BROCKMAN. WE ALREADY PUT OUR *BEST* MAN ON IT.

NO... DON'T TELL ME YOU SENT...*THE MACHINE!*

WE HAD TO. RIGHT ABOUT NOW THE TOUGHEST NEGOTIATOR IN SPRINGFIELD SHOULD BE SITTING DOWN WITH OUR FRIENDS AT SIMP-TV.

IT'S ALMOST TOO CRUEL.

MEANWHILE...

HI, *LIONEL "THE MACHINE" HUTZ,* ATTOR-NEY AT LAW. SO, IT'S LIKE THIS: THE GUYS AT THE NETWORK WANT YOU TO FOLD UP YOUR OPERATION AND STOP BROADCASTING *SIMP-TV.* WHAT DO YOU SAY?

NO.

LOOK, I HAVE TO GO. WE'VE GOT A WHOLE BLOCK OF PRIMETIME SHOWS TO SCRIPT, REHEARSE AND SHOOT BY...WELL, BY PRIMETIME.

OKAY, THEN. THANKS FOR YOUR TIME.

SOON...

SORRY, FELLAS. THE KID'S *TOUGH.*

FELLOW SEMI-CELEBRITIES, THE TIME HAS COME FOR US TO ACT.

THE GUY MAKES 150 MOVIES, AND *NOW* HE DECIDES TO START ACTING.

WHAT'S -HIS-FACE IS *RIGHT*.

THANK YOU, KRUSTY.

PUT A SOCK IN IT! I'M GETTING KILLED IN THE RATINGS. AND NO *RATINGS* MEAN NO *ADVERTISING*. AND NO *ADVERTISING* MEANS NO *MONEY*. AND NO MONEY MEANS...WELL, THAT ONE'S SELF-EXPLANATORY. WHAT ARE WE GOING TO DO ABOUT *SIMP-TV*?

WHAT IF WE FLOOD THEM OUT WITH MY NEW WONDER PRODUCT, "H3O"-- THE WETTEST WATER YOU *EVER* TASTED?

HOW DID *HE* GET IN HERE? HE ISN'T EVEN A SEMI-CELEBRITY.

WELL, HOW MUCH HAIRPAINT HAVE *YOU* SOLD LATELY, CHUMP? THAT MESHUGUNA IS HOCKING MY NEW LINE OF *ARTIFICIAL HIPS*!

FOCUS, PEOPLE. WE'VE GOT TO COME UP WITH SOMETHING TO STOP THESE GUYS AT *SIMP-TV*. THEY'RE TOTALLY TUNED INTO WHAT THE PUBLIC WANTS. IT'S LIKE THEY'RE SUPER-GENIUSES OR SOMETHING.

MEANWHILE, AT THE STUDIO...

WAKE *UP*, BART! WE HAVE AN *EMERGENCY*!

COLONEL KRUST'S 100% CHICK

WHAT? SWING A CRANE IN THERE WITH A DOUBLE-HUNG BOLEX. WE'LL SHOOT IT WITH A SUN GUN AND DUMP DOWN TO HALF-INCH FOR DAILIES.

GET A GRIP, BART. I KNOW YOU'VE BEEN WORKING HARD BUT WE'VE GOT A SITUATION ON OUR HANDS. TAKE A LOOK AT THE *"BAD BOY"* OF *SIMP-TV*!

HEH, HEH...

WHAT ARE YOU TALKING ABOUT? THAT'S CRUEL AND SADISTIC.

HEY, THAT'S NOT BAD.

AND YOUR POINT IS...

BART, THIS WHOLE CHANNEL IS PANDERING TO THE LOWEST COMMON DENOMINATOR IN OUR AUDIENCE. OUTSIDE OF THE AMUSING CONTEXT OF ANIMATED SHOWS AND COMIC BOOKS, THIS KIND OF VIOLENCE IS JUST PLAIN *MEAN*.

BUT IT *SELLS*, SISTER, IT *SELLS*! I'M TAKING THIS CHANNEL TO THE *TOP*, AND I DON'T CARE HOW MANY INNOCENT HEADS GET FLUSHED IN THE PROCESS!

BACK IN THE BOARDROOM...

COME ON, *THINK!* I NEED MY JOB. THE ONLY OTHER THING I'M QUALIFIED FOR IS DITCH-DIGGING, AND THAT'S JUST MURDER ON MY FALLEN ARCHES.

EXCUSE ME, GENTLEMEN, BUT PERHAPS I CAN BE OF SOME ASSISTANCE.

GASP!

AAAAH!

YOU!

I MIGHT HAVE A WAY TO STOP THESE MEDDLESOME MAYHEM-MAKERS RIGHT IN THEIR TRACKS.

BURNS! WHY WOULD *YOU* WANT TO HELP *US*?

YEAH, WOULDN'T IT BE MORE YOUR STYLE TO GO OUT AND *BUY* SIMP-TV AND THEN TRY TO *BURY* US?

THAT'S A HORRIBLE, CYNICAL THING TO SAY, BROCKMAN. BESIDES, THE FCC PROHIBITS ME FROM PURCHASING ANOTHER BROADCAST NETWORK.

THAT REMINDS ME, SMITHERS. WE NEED TO FIND SOME RUBE TO BUY *ZOO-SPAN*. APPARENTLY NO ONE WANTS TO WATCH CAGED ANIMALS SCRATCH THEMSELVES 24 HOURS A DAY.

MONKEYS ARE FUNNY...

OKAY, WHAT'S THE PLAN, BURNS?

I'LL REVEAL MY SCHEME ONLY IF YOU ALL PROMISE TO HAVE ME ON EACH OF YOUR PROGRAMS AS A FEATURED GUEST STAR. PERHAPS YOU DIDN'T KNOW THIS, BUT I CAN TAP DANCE A PRETTY MEAN BUCK AND WING.

I CAN'T WAIT. YOU'RE ON.

DEAL.

OH, WHAT A TANGLED WEB WE WEAVE....*

OKEY DOKEY!

EXCELLENT. YOU SEE, GENTLEMEN, ALL IT TAKES IS A SIMPLE PHONE CALL...

*SIR WALTER SCOTT, THE LAY OF THE LOST MINSTREL, CANTO IV, STANZA 17

AT THE HOME OF REV. AND MRS. LOVEJOY...

STAY TUNED FOR "A VERY BRADY BAPTISM"...

RING-A-RING!

HELLO? YES, INDEED. WHAT? THIS CAN'T BE TRUE! IT'S A SCANDAL!

SWEET BLISTERING ISAIAH, LOVEY! TURN TO CHANNEL 10!

SLAM!

CLICK!

SO THEN I SAID, "IN ALABAMA, THE TUSCALOOSA! GET IT? THE TUSC-A-LOOS-A!

THIS IS AN ABOMINATION! NOT ONLY IS HE MALIGNING THE GREAT BIBLE - BELT STATE OF ALABAMA, BUT THAT'S THE WORST ALAN ALDA IMPRESSION I'VE EVER SEEN! THANK YOU, ANONY-MOUS STRANGER. I'LL TAKE IT FROM HERE.

SIMP-TV

SMITHERS! GET ME MY TAP SHOES.

THUNK!

LATER THAT WEEK...

WELL, SO MUCH FOR BURNS' SURE-FIRE SCHEME.

LOOK AT THE BRIGHT SIDE, FELLAS. AT LEAST WE DON'T HAVE TO PUT HIM ON OUR SHOWS.

TRUE. BUT OUR CAREERS MAY WELL BE OVER.

IT IS A TALE TOLD BY AN IDIOT, FULL OF SOUND AND FURY, SIGNIFYING NOTHING.*

*WILLIAM SHAKESPEARE, MACBETH, ACT 5, SCENE 5

HA, HA!

WHY IS THAT SO FUNNY?

BACK AT THE STUDIO...

I AM TOTALLY EXHAUSTED. YOU KNOW WHAT'S THE WORST PART ABOUT MAKING TV? I DON'T HAVE ANY TIME TO WATCH IT.

YEAH. I HAVEN'T SEEN ANYTHING SINCE SWEEPS. LET'S SEE WHAT'S ON.

CLICK!

OH, MAN. *"ITCHY BLANDINGS BUILDS HIS SCREAM HOUSE"*-- THAT'S A *CLASSIC*.

YEAH--GEMS LIKE THAT COME AROUND BUT ONCE A LIFETIME.

ARE *YOU* THINKING WHAT *I'M* THINKING?

I DON'T KNOW-- ARE YOU THINKING ABOUT HOW MANY LICKS IT TAKES TO GET TO THE CENTER OF A *KRUSTYPOP*?

NO. I'M THINKING THAT WE'VE BEEN WORKING LIKE SLAVES AT SIMP-TV AND NOT REALLY ENJOYING *LIFE*!

YEAH, I GUESS YOU'RE RIGHT. IT WAS *WAY* TOO MUCH HARD WORK, IT MADE US *FIGHT*-- EVEN MORE THAN USUAL--AND WE DIDN'T EARN A *DIME*!

WHAT THE HECK WERE WE *THINKING*?

YEAH. WE MUST HAVE BEEN CRAZY TO THINK *THE SIMPSONS* COULD CHANGE THE FACE OF *TELEVISION*!

BUMBLEBEE MAN IN ¡AY, QUE LASTIMA!

HOW DOTH THE LITTLE BUSY BEE IMPROVE EACH SHINING HOUR, AND GATHER HONEY ALL THE DAY FROM EVERY OPENING FLOWER.[1]

GROMBLE... SMACK-SMACK... MOMBLE...

BLIT BLIT BLIT!!!

BRUSHA BRUSHA BRUSHA!!

MONCH!

GNASH!

CHOMP!

GOLP!

GOBBL!

PAAA!

EXIT BIP!

MEN MUST ENDURE THEIR GOING HENCE, EVEN AS THEIR COMING HITHER.[2]

VRUM!

TUT!

KA-CHUNK!

¡AY, QUE LINDA!*

¡AY, QUE LINDA!

¡TEEHEEHEE!

"OH, HOW PRETTY!"

SIP!

THE HOLLYWOOD VARIETY REPORTER

Hix Nix Big Bug Pix In Stix!

PSST!

PSST!

¡AHORA TE DESTRUIRE, INSECTO ASQUEROSO!*

¡AY, QUE LASTIMA!**

*"NOW I SHALL DESTROY YOU, FOUL INSECT!"
**"OH, HOW HORRIBLE!"

SCRIPT-PENCILS
SCOTT SHAW

TRANSLATION
SERGIO ARAGONES

INKS
BILL MORRISON

LETTERS
JEANNINE CROWELL

COLOR
NATHAN KANE

*TODAY, THE **NATIONAL HEALTH BOARD** ISSUED A WARNING ABOUT THE ALARMING INCREASE IN **INSECT-SPREAD DISEASES**...

*DAMN! I FELL ASLEEP IN THE BEE SUIT AGAIN!

FIN.

1. ISAAC WATTS, *AGAINST IDLENESS AND MISCHIEF*
2. WILLIAM SHAKESPEARE, *KING LEAR*, V.II
3. W.S., *CYMBELINE*, III.II
4. W.S., *AS YOU LIKE IT*, I.III

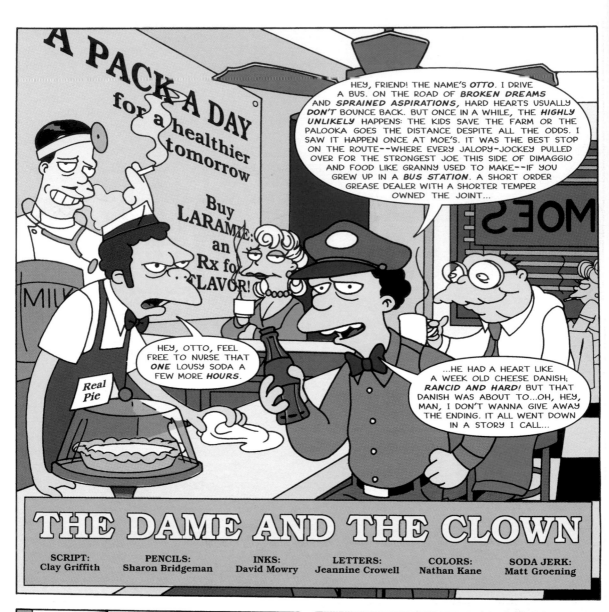

A PACK A DAY for a healthier tomorrow

Buy LARAME: an Rx for FLAVOR!

MILK

Real Pie

HEY, FRIEND! THE NAME'S *OTTO*. I DRIVE A BUS. ON THE ROAD OF *BROKEN DREAMS* AND *SPRAINED ASPIRATIONS*, HARD HEARTS USUALLY *DON'T* BOUNCE BACK. BUT ONCE IN A WHILE, THE *HIGHLY UNLIKELY* HAPPENS: THE KIDS SAVE THE FARM OR THE PALOOKA GOES THE DISTANCE DESPITE ALL THE ODDS. I SAW IT HAPPEN ONCE AT MOE'S. IT WAS THE BEST STOP ON THE ROUTE--WHERE EVERY JALOPY-JOCKEY PULLED OVER FOR THE STRONGEST JOE THIS SIDE OF DIMAGGIO AND FOOD LIKE GRANNY USED TO MAKE--IF YOU GREW UP IN A *BUS STATION*. A SHORT ORDER GREASE DEALER WITH A SHORTER TEMPER OWNED THE JOINT...

MOE'S

HEY, OTTO, FEEL FREE TO NURSE THAT *ONE* LOUSY SODA A FEW MORE *HOURS*.

...HE HAD A HEART LIKE A WEEK OLD CHEESE DANISH; *RANCID AND HARD!* BUT THAT DANISH WAS ABOUT TO...OH, HEY, MAN, I DON'T WANNA GIVE AWAY THE ENDING. IT ALL WENT DOWN IN A STORY I CALL...

THE DAME AND THE CLOWN

SCRIPT:	PENCILS:	INKS:	LETTERS:	COLORS:	SODA JERK:
Clay Griffith	Sharon Bridgeman	David Mowry	Jeannine Crowell	Nathan Kane	Matt Groening

SO LONG, MOE. GOTTA GO REV UP THE REDEYE TO SPRINGFIELD. STAY FROSTY, MAN.

YEAH, THANKS FOR *WEARIN' OUT* MY STOOL!

OH, EXCUSE ME. I DIDN'T SEE YOU THROUGH THE TEARS.

OPEN

WHOA, DOLL! YOU MUST HAVE HAD THE *SCRAPPLE*...

COFFEE, PLEASE.

≳SIGH≲ OKAY.

ALL RIGHT, BUT I DON'T WANT TO HEAR YOUR *PROBLEMS*.

IT'S HOUSE RULES. *NO PROBLEMS*.

I'M GOOD AT SUPPRESSING MY FEELINGS.

Real Pie

OH, MY. WHAT A *LOVELY* PIE CAROUSEL.

REALLY?

YOU REALLY LIKE IT? IT WAS MY *SAINTED MOTHER'S!*

OH, YEAH! SHE LEFT IT TO ME ON HER DEATHBED. "MOE," SHE SAID, "YOU'RE THE ONLY ONE WHO *REALLY* LOVED ME. TAKE THE *PIE THINGY...*"

OH, MA!

THERE, THERE...

ER...UH...*HEY!* DON'T *SOFT-SOAP* ME BY FLATTERING MA'S PIE CAROUSEL.

SORRY. NO OFFENSE.

NOW BOARDING THE 11:15 TO SPRINGFIELD!

OH, HOMER. IF ONLY I COULD AFFORD A TICKET BACK HOME TO YOU.

HEY! I HEARD *THAT!*

I *WARNED* YOU! KEEP IT TO YOURSELF!

Ahoy from your Homey

HEY, *HEY!* UH... I MEAN... *THERE* YOU ARE!

OH, *DEAR!* HE *FOUND* ME!

BABY, I BURNED A LOT OF *BIG SHOE LEATHER* LOOKING FOR *YOU!*

OPE

BIG KRUSTY, *PLEASE*. I'M NOT HAPPY IN CAPITAL CITY.

WHAT DO I KNOW FROM *HAPPY*? I'M A *CLOWN*!

I WANT TO GO BACK TO SPRINGFIELD.

TOUGH DARTS. YOU'RE *MY* MOLL NOW!

WELL...I'M NOT...I'M NOT GOING WITH YOU...

OH, *YEAH*? WE'LL SEE ABOUT THAT!

MMFF! PPPFFF!

WOOO...LIGHT HEADED...GOTTA DRINK MORE *MOXIE*.

SQUEAK

SQUEAK

THIS *INFLATABLE ROSCOE* SAYS YOU'RE COMING WITH ME, SEE?

OH, *DEAR*! WHAT A *VIOLENT* INTERPRETATION OF THE HEARTWARMING CRAFT OF *BALLOON SCULPTURE*!

I *KNEW* THAT DAME WAS GONNA CAUSE ME GRIEF. Y'KNOW?

YEAH, OKAY, WHATEVER...

MAY I HAVE SOME PIE, PLEASE?

RED SKELTON MY *BIG YELLOW BUTT*!

MARGIE! WHERE ARE YOU?

HOLD UP, RINGLING DUDE. CAN'T CROWD THE AISLE WITHOUT A *TICKET*.

WHAT? BUT... BUT...OH, ALL RIGHT.

OY! WHAT A DAY I'M HAVING!

TWO MINUTES LATER...

HEY! HOW 'BOUT WATCHING WHERE I'M GOING, SWEETHEART?

SO LONG, MARGE. GOOD LUCK.

VROOOM!

OH, *GREAT*! NOW I'VE GOT NO MOLL! WHAT AM I GONNA DO? I'M *MOLL-LESS*!

EEYAAAGH!

I'M FREE TONIGHT. WHAT DOES A MOLL DO?

C'MON, I'LL POUR YOU A CUPPA JOE.

YEAH, LIKE I WANT TO STAY UP *NOW*.

HOMER, I'LL *NEVER* STRAY FROM YOU AGAIN!

LOVE *HAPPENS,* MAN! BUT SOMETIMES IT NEEDS A LITTLE HELP. THIS TIME IT CAME FROM A GRISTLED, GRIDDLE-JOCKEY WHO REACHED DOWN INTO HIS GREASE-PIT OF A HEART AND DISCOVERED A PIE BOX FULL OF COMPASSION FOR A DAME IN TROUBLE. MY NAME'S OTTO. I DRIVE A BUS. I'M GOING TO GET A BURRITO.

OH, MARGE... BANANA CREAM! YOU *REMEMBERED*!

FIN.

GET FATTY

C.I.A. HEADQUARTERS
WASHINGTON, D.C.

LETS PLAY A GAME-- I SPY SOMETHING *WEAK* AND *PATHETIC!*

NOT AGAIN!

;CHOKE!;

SCRIPT	PENCILS – ART SUPERVISION	INKS
GARY GLASBERG	STEPHANIE GLADDEN	TIM HARKINS
LETTERS	COLORS	MR. OLYMPIA
JEANNINE CROWELL	NATHAN KANE	MATT GROENING

KNOCK OFF THE *THEATRICS*, WOLFCASTLE! WHO DO YOU THINK *CLEANS UP* THIS MESS EVERY TIME YOU SHOW UP?

BEATS ME. TEAMSTAHS?

GO AHEAD IN. HE'S *EXPECTING* YOU. BUT REMEMBER, DON'T SAY ANYTHING ABOUT HIS WEIGHT OR THAT INCIDENT WHEN YOU...

• PRESIDENT •

SLAM!

HIYA, *TUBBY!* I HAVEN'T SEEN YOU SINCE *OCTOBAHFEST* AT *CAMP DAVID* WHEN *TOMMY TUNE* AND *I* STOPPED YOU FROM DOING *"SINGING IN DA RAIN"* UNDAH DA BIDET!

SIT DOWN, RAINIER. WE HAVE A CRISIS ON OUR HANDS THAT POSES A *SEVERE THREAT* TO NATIONAL SECURITY.

CHOMP! CHOMP!

DA ONLY TING I SEE ON YOUR HANDS, MR. PRESIDENT, IS *SPECIAL SAUCE*.

USING OUR OWN SURVEILLANCE SATELLITES, WE'VE DETECTED SOMETHING *TRULY HORRIFYING* RIGHT HERE IN OUR OWN BACKYARD!

I KNOW, I KNOW. DAT *MOESHA* SHOW IS TOTALLY OUT OF CONTROL.

DEEP IN THE HEART OF THIS GREAT LAND, LIES A COMMUNITY WHOSE CITIZENS APPEAR TO PRIDE THEMSELVES ON *OVER-INDULGENCE*...

EMBARRASSING THEMSELVES...

AND HAVING THE *WORST* CHOLESTEROL COUNT IN MODERN HISTORY!

RAINIER, AS FITNESS AMBASSADOR, I NEED YOU TO TAKE ON SPRINGFIELD'S WORST OFFENDERS AND WHIP THEM INTO SHAPE. OUR NATION NEEDS YOUR HELP!

NORMALLY, I'D HAVE TO PASS, BUT DEY JUST PUSHED BACK THE SHOOTING SCHEDULE FOR MY *NEW MUSICAL*, "MCBAINIE GET YOUR GUN."

HAVE MY SECRETARY HOLD MY CALLS--IT'S TIME TO KICK SOME *CELLULITE*.

LATER...

LYDIA, DID I...AH... GET ANY CALLS?

JUST THE *PRESIDENT*, SIR.

TELL HIM TO MAKE THE CHECK OUT TO "*CASH!*"

I DON'T THINK THAT'S WHAT HE'S CALLING ABOUT, SIR. WE SEEM TO BE UNDER SOME KIND OF *ASSAULT*.

THE CITY'S PANICKING, MR. MAYOR.

THERE'S A *RIOT* AT THE BOWLING ALLEY-- THE SNACK BAR'S SERVING *STEAMED VEGETABLES!*

I KNEW THERE'D BE A *VEGAN REVOLT* SOMEDAY! BLASTED HEALTH FREAKS! I WANT THE...ERR.. NATIONAL GUARD TO SURROUND EVERY HOT DOG CART AND CHEESE STEAK JOINT IN THE CITY. CHUNKY PEOPLE MEAN CHUNKY DONATIONS!

IF THAT DOESN'T WORK, CALL...

SMASH!

KRACK!

WOLFCASTLE!!

BY *ORDER* OF DA *PRESIDENT*, QUIMBY, LET'S TALK *LOWFAT TURKEY!*

LATER...

I'M *STARVED*, MAN! WHAT'S FOR LUNCH?

I THINK IT'S BAKED BEANS DAY.

:SIGH: ...WHEN WILL THEY *LEARN*?

AN ORDER OF *FRENCH FRIES* AND DON'T BE *STINGY* WITH THE *LIPIDS*, MY GOOD WOMAN.

STUFF IT, KID. NO MORE *FRIED FOOD*. FROM NOW ON, WE ONLY SERVE MCBAIN'S POWDERED PROTEIN SMOOTHIES. *TAKE 'EM OR LEAVE 'EM!*

GULP GULP GULP

BLECH!

HACK

GURP!

GAG

ELSEWHERE...

ENERGY LEVELS... NEARLY *DEPLETED*... EFFECTS OF BREAKFAST WEARING *OFF*...

PLAC TRA HE

EMERGENCY SYRUP PACKET *UNOPENABLE* IN CURRENT *WEAKENED* STATE...

COMPANY-SUPPLIED CARBOS WITHIN REACH... *MUST HANG ON...*

CRUUUD!!!

Crudités Here to Stay!

LATER...

HAND OVER THE REMOTE, LISA. THERE'S A GREAT *FOREIGN FILM* ON CHANNEL FIVE!

SINCE WHEN ARE *YOU* INTERESTED IN FOREIGN FILMS?

SNATCH!

SINCE THE CRITICALLY-ACCLAIMED RELEASE OF *"LIKE WATER FOR BRATWURST."*

AND NOW, A *SPECIAL REPORT* FROM CITY HALL.

GOOD PEOPLE OF SPRINGFIELD, LAY DOWN YOUR *CORN DOGS* AND *COCONUT SNOWBALLS* AND... ER...LISTEN TO ME.

THAT MEANS *YOU*, JUMBO!

D'OH!

UNCLE SAM NEEDS YOU TO FACE YOUR GREATEST ADVERSARY...THE MIGHTY *MID-SECTION*...THE *CELLULITE* ASSASSINS...*THE BIG BUTT BRIGADE!*

THE PEOPLE ON THIS LIST HAVE CAUSED SPRINGFIELD TO BE VOTED THE MOST *UNHEALTHY* CITY IN *HISTORY*. THEREFORE, THE WORST WEIGHT OFFENDERS HAVE *TWO WEEKS* TO LOSE *TEN POUNDS*. IF YOU'RE SUCCESSFUL, THE PRESIDENT WILL REWARD OUR FAIR CITY WITH A *WATER PARK* FOR YOUR... AH...SUMMER ENJOYMENT. IF YOU FAIL...

CHIEF CLANCY WIGGUM
BARNEY GUMBLE
DR. JULIUS HIBBERT
RALPH WIGGUM
NELSON MUNTZ
ABE SIMPSON
HOMER SIMPSON
APU NAHASPEEMAPETILON
KRUSTY THE CLOWN
MARTIN PRINCE
KENT BROCKMAN

YOU'LL SPEND *ONE YEAR* AT *SHELBYVILLE MAXIMUM SECURITY FAT FARM!*

OH, DEAR! THE SITE OF THE *GREAT CRULLER UPRISING* OF 1982! TO THIS DAY, THEY HAVEN'T BEEN ABLE TO REMOVE THE *GREASE STAINS* FROM THE WALLS!

LAY OFF THE SNICKERDOODLES, HOMER, OR YOU'LL BECOME KNOWN AS "THE FAT MAN OF ALCATRAZ!"

WHY YOU LITTLE...!

FATTICA! FATTICA!

DAY ONE...

THEY'RE NOT HEAVY, THEY'RE MY BRETHREN

WELL, CLIP MY COOKIE DUSTER! *LOOK* AT THIS TURNOUT!

I HAVEN'T SEEN DIS MANY LARDBOTTOMS SINCE I JUDGED THE "BOSS HOGG LOOK-ALIKE CONTEST" IN '81!

I'M OK YOU'RE NOT

I WANT TO THANK ALL YOU FOLKS FOR COMING TO TODAY'S BIG CHURCHGOERS AEROBICS CLASS.

THERE'S NOTHING LIKE A WORKOUT TO THE BEST OF BURL IVES!

OH, JIMMY CRACK CORN, AND I DON'T CARE...

DAY TWO...

ALL RIGHT, MEN. ARE YOU READY?

ACH! WHATTA YE *WAITIN'* FER? DYOO IT! *NAB* THE *PORKER!*

El Barto

STOP HIM! THE LAD'S FLUSHING THE EVIDENCE!

KVUMP!

DAY THREE...

:SIGH:

...DO YOU FEEL ANYTHING YET, SELMA?

I'M *EXHAUSTED.* HOW ABOUT A *CIGA-RETTE* BREAK?

NO TIME FOR *BUTTS,* LADIES! YOU TWO GOT MORE *BUTT* DAN YOU NEED *ALREADY!*

DAY FOUR...

TEN MORE MILES, WIGGUM. YOU CAN DO IT!

KEEP YOUR EYES ON THE PRIZE!

0.2 MPH

I LOVE THE SMELL OF SWEAT AND ANCHOVIES IN THE MORNING! SMELLS LIKE... *SWEATY ANCHOVIES!*

I SWEAR, MR. DEVIL, I TRIED TO LOSE THE TEN POUNDS... *REALLY!*

BUT WHEN I SAW THAT *HONEY-GLAZED BEARCLAW*, I...

ENOUGH! SIMPSON, YOU ARE SENTENCED TO BE *BURNED* AT THE *STAKE*. HOW DO YOU PLEAD?

MMM...STEAK!

POOF!

WHAT A *TASTY* DREAM! I'M STARVED!

I WONDER IF THERE'S ANY *MU-SHU PORK* LEFT OVER FROM DINNER?

CLICK!

AAAAH!

DERE'S NO SUCH TING AS A "LO *MEIN*-TENANCE DIET," CHUBBY!

THINK FAST, SIMPSON!

HE'S *SLEEPWALKING*, SIR. SHOULD WE WAKE HIM?

AND RISK GETTING *SUED* IF HE HAS A *HAHT ATTACK*?! MY *LAWYAH'S* GOT *ENOUGH* TROUBLE!

DAY FIVE...

YO, LISA! WHAT'S THE BIG HOLD UP?!

HAVEN'T YOU HEARD, OTTO? KRUSTY'S SELLING "*SOY GOY: THE KOSHER VEGETARIAN BURGER.*"

WHO WANTS *AVOCADO* AND *EXTRA SPROUTS*? THERE'S PLENTY FOR ALL YOU *SALAD-HAPPY SAPS*!

CHING!

ELSEWHERE...

HEY, APU. GIVE ME A COTTON CANDY FLAVORED SQUISHEE AND A "HEART STOPPER" 14-LAYER MICROWAVE BURRITO.

NO CAN DO, BART. WE ARE ONLY SELLING *WHEATGRASS SQUISHEES* NOW. HOW WOULD YOU LIKE ONE WITH *EXTRA BEE POLLEN*?

THWACK!

THE DAY I *PRAYED* WOULD NEVER COME IS *UPON US*...

YOU GAINED THREE POUNDS, *FATSO.*

HISS!

BOO!

FATSO!

BOO!

HISS!

BOO!

YA LOSER!

GET OUT OF TOWN, SIMPSON! YOU'RE *RUINING* IT FOR ALL OF US!

IF YOU EVER COME NEAR MY *BEER NUTS* AGAIN, HOMER, I'LL *KILL* YA!

THERE, THERE NEIGHBOR. I KNOW JUST HOW YOU FEEL.

I HAVE THE DARNDEST TIME CONTROLLING *MY* HABIT OF COMFORTING PEOPLE AT *INAPPROPRIATE TIMES.*

ACH, YE SHOULD'VE TRIED MY *HAGGIS AND GRAPEFRUIT DIET!*

NOT SO FAST, MAN. AS *EASY* AS IT IS TO STAND "BEHIND" YOU, WE'VE GOT SOMETHING TO SAY!

THE SIMPSON FAMILY IS A *TEAM*, DAD, BUT YOU LET US DOWN!

SHAPE UP, HOMER. IF YOU DON'T WANT TO DO IT FOR THE TOWN, DO IT FOR *US* INSTEAD!

BUT LOOK AT ME! HOW CAN I LOSE *THIRTEEN POUNDS* IN ONE WEEK?! I'LL HAVE TO RESORT TO SOME KIND OF *APPETITE SUPPRESSANT!*

NO PROBLEMO, DUDE!

BEHOLD! A PHOTO OF AUNT PATTY AND AUNT SELMA WHEN THEY WON THAT *LADY LARAMIE HARD BODIES BIKINI CONTEST!*

YEEEAAA!

GOOD WORK, BOY!

I, HOMER SIMPSON, WILL *LOSE WEIGHT*.

I WILL MAKE MY FRIENDS AND FAMILY PROUD!!

MOMENTS LATER...

HELLO, COLIN... DON'T TELL DA MRS., BUT HOW WOULD YOU LIKE TO BE MY *VICE PRESIDENT* IN DA YEAR 2000?

KRASH!

MCBAIN, GET YOUR *WATER-WRINKLED BICEPS* OUT OF THE TUB. WE'VE GOT *SERIOUS* WORK TO DO!

DAY EIGHT...

FROM DIS POINT ON, SIMPSON, YOU AH A *MACHINE*.

DAY NINE...

BRAAAP!

YOU *EAT, SLEEP,* AND CA-CA FITNESS!

DAY TEN...

EYE OF DA *TIGER!* NO *PAIN,* NO *GAIN!* FEEL DA BURN, *LAHD RUMP!*

DAY ELEVEN...

YOU AH *STRONG*...

DAY TWELVE...

YOU AH *INVINCIBLE*...

DAY THIRTEEN...

YOU AH *HOMAH*!!!!

HOUSE-O-DONUTS

IN YOUR *FACE*, TASTY BREAKFAST TREAT!

DAY FOURTEEN...

WELL...AH...SIMPSON, *EVERYONE'S* WEIGHED IN. IT'S ALL UP TO *YOU*.

GOOD LUCK, *HOMAH*.

IF IT DOESN'T WORK OUT, YOU CAN COME WORK FOR ME IN *HOLLYWOOD*. I NEED SOMEONE TO *CLEAN* DA *STALLS* OF MY *LLAMA RANCH*!

MAYBE I SHOULDN'T HAVE EATEN THAT *GREEN BEAN* FOR DINNER LAST NIGHT!

DON'T WORRY, HOMEY. REMEMBER, WE *BELIEVE* IN YOU!

;GULP!;

240 250 260

;GASP!;

12 POUNDS, 15 OUNCES...YOU *DIDN'T* MAKE IT, SIMPSON!

EDITOR'S NOTE:
NOT A RECOMMENDED
METHOD OF WEIGHT LOSS!

BART'S PAL,

Milhouse

#1

BONGO

2ND BANANA

MILHOUSE
IN
"THE QUEST FOR YAZ"

OKAY, I'VE *FINALLY* SAVED UP ENOUGH FOR THE 1973 CARL YASTZREMSKI "MUTTON CHOP YAZ" BASEBALL CARD. HAND OVER THOSE SWEET SIDEBURNS!

NOT LIKELY. YOU SEE, THE $30 IN YOUR *LESS-THAN-TIDY* HANDS REFLECTS ONLY *HALF* THE CURRENT VALUE OF YE OLDE MUTTON CHOP YAZ.

DO I LOOK LIKE *I* CONTROL THE BASEBALL CARD MARKET? I THINK NOT.

WUH? BUT YOU SAID IT WAS $30.

THE INVISIBLE HAND OF THE MARKETPLACE WORKS IN UNPREDICTABLE, BUT PROFITABLE WAYS. AND SAID INVISIBLE HAND HAS DEEMED THAT *YOU* HAVE TO COUGH UP 60 *BONES* BEFORE YOU SEE SIDEBURN ONE.

YOU BREAK THE FOIL STAMP YOU'VE BOUGHT IT!!

YOU MUST BE THIS TALL

$100

I DON'T KNOW ABOUT ANY "INVISIBLE HANDS," BUT THAT SOUNDS LIKE *PRICE GOUGING* TO ME.

THAT'S IT! BY YOUR USE OF THE "G" WORD YOU HAVE BESMIRCHED THE GOOD NAME OF THE ANDROID'S DUNGEON. I HATE TO DO THIS, BUT RULES ARE RULES...

SHWOK!

VREE-EEEE!

HEY!

BANNED FOR LIFE

CONGRATULATIONS. YOU ARE NOW *BANNED FOR LIFE* FROM THIS ESTABLISHMENT.

AND THIS IS THE *MLB* "BANNED FOR LIFE." NOT THE SISSY *NBA* OR *NFL* KIND, WHERE A QUICK JAUNT TO THE TREMBLING HILLS CLINIC WILL GET YOU BACK IN. NOW, *VACATE* THE PREMISES BEFORE I RUN YOU THROUGH WITH MY OFFICIALLY LICENSED D&D *DIE-CAST BROADSWORD*.

AWW, *PLEASE* GIMME A SECOND CHANCE!

WHO NEEDS HIS CRUMMY OLD STORE ANYWAY? SOMEDAY, THE KIDS OF SPRINGFIELD WILL DISCOVER *MAIL-ORDER*, AND THEN *HE'LL* BE SORRY.

OPEN

I HEARD THAT!

WOW! MY VERY OWN *YAZ CARD!* WAIT 'TIL BART SEES *THIS!* NEXT TO THAT KID WHO GOT THE WILLIE DIPKIN "FISHFACE" CARD FOR CHRISTMAS, I'M THE *HAPPIEST* GUY IN SPRINGFIELD.

ARE YOU *REALLY?*

WHO *SAID* THAT?

I DID. I'M *HERE*--IN YOUR BACK POCKET.

MUTTON CHOP YAZ!? WOW, A BASEBALL CARD THAT CAN *TALK!*

I CAN'T *REALLY* TALK. THIS IS JUST A DAYDREAM FORCED UPON YOU BY YOUR *GUILT-RIDDEN* CONSCIENCE.

BUT I ONLY STOLE YOU 'CAUSE I'M YOUR BIGGEST FAN. I'VE BEEN WAITING MY *WHOLE LIFE* FOR YOU.

NO *TRUE* FAN OF MINE WOULD STEAL TO GET MY BASEBALL CARD.

THE PROPER SOURCE FOR BASEBALL CARDS IS ANY OF THE SEEMINGLY *ENDLESS* STRING OF BASEBALL CARD SHOPS. THEIR UNABASHED PROFITEERING HAS BECOME AS AMERICAN AS APPLE PIE AND FREE AGENCY.

CARL YASTRZEMSKI
BOSTON RED SOX

I S'POSE YOU'RE RIGHT. I KNEW SOMETHING WAS BOTHERING ME, BUT I JUST THOUGHT I DRANK MY *TANDOORI CHICKEN FLAVORED SQUISHEE* TOO FAST. I GUESS IT MUST BE THE GUILT.

THERE'S ONLY ONE WAY TO UNBURDEN YOUR CONSCIENCE. YOU MUST *RETURN ME* TO MY RIGHTFUL PLACE IN THE SPOKES OF RALPH'S BICYCLE.

LATER, AT THE WIGGUM HOUSE...

IF CHIEF WIGGUM AND RALPH KEEP PLAYING FETCH, THEY WON'T SEE ME SNEAKING IN THE BACK.

CRASH!

OUCH!

ADAM FEIN
SCRIPT

CHRIS ROMAN
PENCILS

TIM BAVINGTON
INKS

JEANNINE CROWELL
LETTERS

PETER ALEXANDER
COLORS

MATT GROENING
THE GREEN MONSTER